50 Hearty Soups for Chilly Nights

By: Kelly Johnson

Table of Contents

- Chicken Noodle Soup
- Beef Stew
- Creamy Tomato Basil Soup
- Vegetable Lentil Soup
- Split Pea Soup
- Minestrone Soup
- Potato Leek Soup
- Butternut Squash Soup
- Chili con Carne
- French Onion Soup
- Creamy Mushroom Soup
- Clam Chowder
- Tuscan White Bean Soup
- Corn Chowder
- Beef Barley Soup
- Chicken Tortilla Soup
- Wild Rice and Mushroom Soup
- Curried Pumpkin Soup
- Cabbage Roll Soup
- Italian Sausage and Kale Soup
- Sausage and Lentil Soup
- Spicy Black Bean Soup
- Coconut Curry Chicken Soup
- Creamy Broccoli Cheddar Soup
- Savory Beef and Potato Soup
- Shrimp and Corn Chowder
- Chicken and Wild Rice Soup
- Sweet Potato and Black Bean Soup
- Mediterranean Chickpea Soup
- Borscht (Beet Soup)
- Pho (Vietnamese Noodle Soup)
- Chicken and Dumpling Soup
- Egg Drop Soup
- Roasted Garlic and Cauliflower Soup
- Kale and Quinoa Soup

- Seafood Gumbo
- Spicy Thai Soup (Tom Yum)
- Ham and Bean Soup
- Pasta Fagioli
- Zucchini and Tomato Soup
- Chicken Pho
- Spaghetti and Meatball Soup
- Vegetable and Barley Soup
- Beef and Cabbage Soup
- Cheesy Potato Soup
- Lemon Chicken Orzo Soup
- Carrot Ginger Soup
- Tuscan Kale and Sausage Soup
- Stuffed Pepper Soup
- Lentil and Spinach Soup

Chicken Noodle Soup

Ingredients

- 1 tablespoon olive oil
- 1 onion, diced
- 2 carrots, sliced
- 2 celery stalks, sliced
- 3 cloves garlic, minced
- 8 cups chicken broth
- 2 cups cooked chicken, shredded
- 1 teaspoon dried thyme
- 1 bay leaf
- 2 cups egg noodles
- Salt and pepper to taste
- Fresh parsley, chopped (for garnish)

Instructions

1. **Sauté Vegetables:**
    - In a large pot, heat olive oil over medium heat. Add onion, carrots, and celery. Sauté until softened, about 5 minutes. Add garlic and cook for an additional minute.
2. **Add Broth and Chicken:**
    - Pour in the chicken broth and bring to a boil. Stir in the shredded chicken, thyme, and bay leaf. Reduce heat and simmer for 20 minutes.
3. **Cook Noodles:**
    - Add the egg noodles and cook according to package instructions until tender. Season with salt and pepper to taste.
4. **Serve:**
    - Remove the bay leaf, garnish with fresh parsley, and serve hot.

Beef Stew

Ingredients

- 2 pounds beef chuck, cut into 1-inch cubes
- 3 tablespoons vegetable oil
- 1 onion, chopped
- 3 carrots, sliced
- 3 potatoes, diced
- 4 cups beef broth
- 2 tablespoons tomato paste
- 2 teaspoons dried thyme
- 1 teaspoon garlic powder
- Salt and pepper to taste
- 2 bay leaves

Instructions

1. **Brown the Beef:**
    - In a large pot, heat oil over medium-high heat. Add beef cubes and brown on all sides. Remove beef and set aside.
2. **Sauté Vegetables:**
    - In the same pot, add onion, carrots, and potatoes. Cook until slightly softened. Stir in tomato paste, thyme, garlic powder, salt, and pepper.
3. **Simmer:**
    - Return the beef to the pot and add beef broth and bay leaves. Bring to a boil, then reduce heat and let simmer for about 1.5 to 2 hours, or until beef is tender.
4. **Serve:**
    - Remove bay leaves and serve hot with crusty bread.

Creamy Tomato Basil Soup

Ingredients

- 2 tablespoons olive oil
- 1 onion, chopped
- 3 cloves garlic, minced
- 2 cans (28 ounces each) crushed tomatoes
- 2 cups vegetable broth
- 1 cup heavy cream
- 1/2 cup fresh basil, chopped
- Salt and pepper to taste

Instructions

1. **Sauté Aromatics:**
    - In a large pot, heat olive oil over medium heat. Add onion and cook until translucent. Add garlic and sauté for another minute.
2. **Add Tomatoes and Broth:**
    - Stir in crushed tomatoes and vegetable broth. Bring to a simmer and cook for 15 minutes.
3. **Blend and Add Cream:**
    - Use an immersion blender to puree the soup until smooth. Stir in heavy cream and basil, and season with salt and pepper.
4. **Serve:**
    - Heat through and serve with fresh basil on top.

Vegetable Lentil Soup

Ingredients

- 2 tablespoons olive oil
- 1 onion, chopped
- 2 carrots, diced
- 2 celery stalks, diced
- 3 cloves garlic, minced
- 1 cup lentils (green or brown), rinsed
- 6 cups vegetable broth
- 1 can (14.5 ounces) diced tomatoes
- 1 teaspoon cumin
- 1 teaspoon thyme
- Salt and pepper to taste
- 2 cups spinach (optional)

Instructions

1. **Sauté Vegetables:**
    - In a large pot, heat olive oil over medium heat. Add onion, carrots, and celery. Cook until softened. Stir in garlic and cook for an additional minute.
2. **Add Lentils and Broth:**
    - Add lentils, vegetable broth, diced tomatoes, cumin, thyme, salt, and pepper. Bring to a boil, then reduce heat and simmer for about 30-35 minutes or until lentils are tender.
3. **Finish:**
    - If using spinach, stir it in during the last 5 minutes of cooking. Adjust seasoning as needed.
4. **Serve:**
    - Ladle into bowls and serve warm.

Split Pea Soup

Ingredients

- 2 cups split peas, rinsed
- 1 tablespoon olive oil
- 1 onion, chopped
- 2 carrots, diced
- 2 celery stalks, diced
- 4 cups vegetable broth
- 2 bay leaves
- 1 teaspoon thyme
- Salt and pepper to taste

Instructions

1. **Sauté Vegetables:**
   - In a large pot, heat olive oil over medium heat. Add onion, carrots, and celery. Sauté until softened.
2. **Add Split Peas:**
   - Stir in the split peas, vegetable broth, bay leaves, thyme, salt, and pepper. Bring to a boil.
3. **Simmer:**
   - Reduce heat and let simmer for about 1.5 hours or until peas are tender. Stir occasionally.
4. **Blend (Optional):**
   - For a creamier texture, blend part of the soup with an immersion blender.
5. **Serve:**
   - Remove bay leaves and serve hot.

Minestrone Soup

Ingredients

- 2 tablespoons olive oil
- 1 onion, chopped
- 2 carrots, diced
- 2 celery stalks, diced
- 3 cloves garlic, minced
- 1 can (14.5 ounces) diced tomatoes
- 6 cups vegetable broth
- 1 can (15 ounces) kidney beans, drained and rinsed
- 1 cup pasta (small shapes)
- 2 cups chopped seasonal vegetables (e.g., zucchini, green beans)
- 1 teaspoon Italian seasoning
- Salt and pepper to taste
- Fresh parsley, chopped (for garnish)

Instructions

1. **Sauté Aromatics:**
    - In a large pot, heat olive oil over medium heat. Add onion, carrots, and celery. Cook until softened. Stir in garlic and cook for an additional minute.
2. **Add Vegetables and Broth:**
    - Add diced tomatoes, vegetable broth, kidney beans, pasta, seasonal vegetables, Italian seasoning, salt, and pepper. Bring to a boil.
3. **Simmer:**
    - Reduce heat and let simmer for about 20-25 minutes or until pasta is tender.
4. **Serve:**
    - Garnish with fresh parsley and serve hot.

Potato Leek Soup

Ingredients

- 2 tablespoons olive oil
- 3 leeks, cleaned and sliced
- 2 potatoes, peeled and diced
- 4 cups vegetable broth
- 1 cup heavy cream (optional)
- Salt and pepper to taste
- Chives or parsley for garnish

Instructions

1. **Sauté Leeks:**
   - In a large pot, heat olive oil over medium heat. Add sliced leeks and cook until softened.
2. **Add Potatoes and Broth:**
   - Stir in diced potatoes and vegetable broth. Bring to a boil, then reduce heat and simmer for 20-25 minutes until potatoes are tender.
3. **Blend and Finish:**
   - Use an immersion blender to puree the soup until smooth. Stir in heavy cream (if using), and season with salt and pepper.
4. **Serve:**
   - Garnish with chives or parsley before serving.

Butternut Squash Soup

Ingredients

- 1 butternut squash, peeled and cubed
- 1 onion, chopped
- 2 carrots, diced
- 3 cloves garlic, minced
- 4 cups vegetable broth
- 1 teaspoon ground cinnamon
- Salt and pepper to taste
- 1/2 cup coconut milk (optional)
- Pumpkin seeds for garnish (optional)

Instructions

1. **Sauté Vegetables:**
    - In a large pot, heat olive oil over medium heat. Add onion, carrots, and garlic. Sauté until softened.
2. **Add Squash and Broth:**
    - Stir in cubed butternut squash, vegetable broth, cinnamon, salt, and pepper. Bring to a boil, then reduce heat and simmer for about 25-30 minutes until squash is tender.
3. **Blend and Finish:**
    - Use an immersion blender to puree the soup until smooth. Stir in coconut milk (if using).
4. **Serve:**
    - Garnish with pumpkin seeds and serve hot.

Chili con Carne

Ingredients

- 2 tablespoons olive oil
- 1 onion, chopped
- 2 cloves garlic, minced
- 1 pound ground beef (or turkey)
- 1 can (15 ounces) kidney beans, drained and rinsed
- 1 can (15 ounces) black beans, drained and rinsed
- 1 can (28 ounces) crushed tomatoes
- 2 tablespoons chili powder
- 1 teaspoon cumin
- 1 teaspoon paprika
- Salt and pepper to taste
- Optional toppings: shredded cheese, sour cream, chopped green onions

Instructions

1. **Sauté Aromatics:**
   - In a large pot, heat olive oil over medium heat. Add onion and garlic; sauté until onion is translucent.
2. **Brown the Meat:**
   - Add the ground beef to the pot and cook until browned. Drain excess fat.
3. **Add Beans and Tomatoes:**
   - Stir in the kidney beans, black beans, crushed tomatoes, chili powder, cumin, paprika, salt, and pepper. Bring to a boil.
4. **Simmer:**
   - Reduce heat and let simmer for at least 30 minutes, stirring occasionally.
5. **Serve:**
   - Ladle into bowls and top with your choice of shredded cheese, sour cream, or green onions.

French Onion Soup

Ingredients

- 4 large onions, thinly sliced
- 2 tablespoons butter
- 1 tablespoon olive oil
- 1 teaspoon sugar
- 4 cups beef broth
- 1 cup white wine (or additional broth)
- 2 teaspoons thyme (fresh or dried)
- Salt and pepper to taste
- Baguette slices, toasted
- Gruyère cheese, shredded

Instructions

1. **Caramelize Onions:**
   - In a large pot, melt butter with olive oil over medium heat. Add sliced onions and sugar; cook until caramelized, about 25-30 minutes.
2. **Add Broth and Wine:**
   - Stir in beef broth, white wine, thyme, salt, and pepper. Bring to a boil and then reduce heat to simmer for 20 minutes.
3. **Prepare Bread:**
   - Preheat your broiler. Ladle soup into oven-safe bowls, top with toasted baguette slices, and sprinkle with Gruyère cheese.
4. **Broil:**
   - Place bowls under the broiler until the cheese is bubbly and golden.
5. **Serve:**
   - Carefully remove from oven and serve hot.

Creamy Mushroom Soup

Ingredients

- 2 tablespoons butter
- 1 onion, chopped
- 3 cloves garlic, minced
- 1 pound mushrooms, sliced (any variety)
- 4 cups vegetable broth
- 1 cup heavy cream
- 1 teaspoon thyme
- Salt and pepper to taste
- Fresh parsley for garnish

Instructions

1. **Sauté Aromatics:**
   - In a large pot, melt butter over medium heat. Add onion and garlic; sauté until soft.
2. **Cook Mushrooms:**
   - Add sliced mushrooms and cook until browned and tender. Season with thyme, salt, and pepper.
3. **Add Broth:**
   - Pour in vegetable broth and bring to a boil. Reduce heat and simmer for 15 minutes.
4. **Blend and Finish:**
   - Use an immersion blender to puree the soup to your desired consistency. Stir in heavy cream and heat through.
5. **Serve:**
   - Garnish with fresh parsley and serve hot.

Clam Chowder

Ingredients

- 4 strips of bacon, diced
- 1 onion, chopped
- 2 celery stalks, diced
- 2 cloves garlic, minced
- 2 cups potatoes, diced
- 2 cans (6.5 ounces each) chopped clams (with juice)
- 2 cups clam juice
- 1 cup heavy cream
- 1 teaspoon thyme
- Salt and pepper to taste
- Fresh parsley for garnish

Instructions

1. **Cook Bacon:**
    - In a large pot, cook bacon over medium heat until crispy. Remove bacon and set aside, leaving the drippings in the pot.
2. **Sauté Vegetables:**
    - Add onion, celery, and garlic to the pot. Sauté until onion is translucent.
3. **Add Potatoes and Liquids:**
    - Stir in diced potatoes, clams (with juice), clam juice, and thyme. Bring to a boil, then reduce heat and simmer until potatoes are tender.
4. **Finish with Cream:**
    - Stir in heavy cream and season with salt and pepper. Cook for a few more minutes.
5. **Serve:**
    - Garnish with cooked bacon and fresh parsley before serving hot.

Tuscan White Bean Soup

Ingredients

- 2 tablespoons olive oil
- 1 onion, chopped
- 2 carrots, diced
- 2 celery stalks, diced
- 3 cloves garlic, minced
- 4 cups vegetable broth
- 2 cans (15 ounces each) white beans (cannellini or great northern), drained and rinsed
- 1 can (14.5 ounces) diced tomatoes
- 1 teaspoon dried rosemary
- 1 teaspoon thyme
- Salt and pepper to taste
- Fresh spinach or kale (optional)

Instructions

1. **Sauté Vegetables:**
   - In a large pot, heat olive oil over medium heat. Add onion, carrots, and celery; sauté until softened. Add garlic and cook for an additional minute.
2. **Add Broth and Beans:**
   - Stir in vegetable broth, white beans, diced tomatoes, rosemary, thyme, salt, and pepper. Bring to a boil.
3. **Simmer:**
   - Reduce heat and simmer for 20-30 minutes. If using spinach or kale, stir it in during the last 5 minutes.
4. **Serve:**
   - Ladle into bowls and serve hot.

Corn Chowder

Ingredients

- 4 strips of bacon, diced
- 1 onion, chopped
- 2 cups potatoes, diced
- 4 cups corn (fresh, frozen, or canned)
- 4 cups vegetable broth
- 1 cup heavy cream
- Salt and pepper to taste
- Chives or parsley for garnish

Instructions

1. **Cook Bacon:**
    - In a large pot, cook bacon over medium heat until crispy. Remove bacon and set aside, leaving drippings in the pot.
2. **Sauté Onion:**
    - Add onion to the pot and sauté until translucent.
3. **Add Potatoes and Corn:**
    - Stir in potatoes, corn, and vegetable broth. Bring to a boil, then reduce heat and simmer until potatoes are tender.
4. **Finish with Cream:**
    - Stir in heavy cream, and season with salt and pepper. Heat through.
5. **Serve:**
    - Garnish with cooked bacon and fresh herbs before serving hot.

Beef Barley Soup

Ingredients

- 1 pound beef stew meat, cubed
- 2 tablespoons olive oil
- 1 onion, chopped
- 2 carrots, diced
- 2 celery stalks, diced
- 3 cloves garlic, minced
- 6 cups beef broth
- 1 cup barley
- 1 teaspoon thyme
- Salt and pepper to taste

Instructions

1. **Brown the Meat:**
    - In a large pot, heat olive oil over medium heat. Add cubed beef and brown on all sides. Remove beef and set aside.
2. **Sauté Vegetables:**
    - In the same pot, add onion, carrots, and celery. Sauté until softened. Stir in garlic and cook for an additional minute.
3. **Add Beef and Broth:**
    - Return beef to the pot and add beef broth, barley, thyme, salt, and pepper. Bring to a boil.
4. **Simmer:**
    - Reduce heat and let simmer for about 1.5 hours or until beef is tender and barley is cooked.
5. **Serve:**
    - Ladle into bowls and serve hot.

Chicken Tortilla Soup

Ingredients

- 2 tablespoons olive oil
- 1 onion, chopped
- 2 cloves garlic, minced
- 1 can (14.5 ounces) diced tomatoes
- 4 cups chicken broth
- 1 can (15 ounces) black beans, drained and rinsed
- 1 cup corn (fresh or frozen)
- 2 cups cooked chicken, shredded
- 1 teaspoon cumin
- Salt and pepper to taste
- Tortilla chips, avocado, and cilantro for garnish

Instructions

1. **Sauté Aromatics:**
    - In a large pot, heat olive oil over medium heat. Add onion and garlic; sauté until softened.
2. **Add Tomatoes and Broth:**
    - Stir in diced tomatoes, chicken broth, black beans, corn, shredded chicken, cumin, salt, and pepper. Bring to a boil.
3. **Simmer:**
    - Reduce heat and let simmer for 20 minutes.
4. **Serve:**
    - Ladle into bowls and garnish with tortilla chips, avocado, and cilantro.

Wild Rice and Mushroom Soup

Ingredients

- 2 tablespoons olive oil
- 1 onion, chopped
- 3 cloves garlic, minced
- 1 cup mushrooms, sliced
- 4 cups vegetable broth
- 1 cup wild rice, rinsed
- 2 cups spinach (optional)
- 1 teaspoon thyme
- Salt and pepper to taste

Instructions

1. **Sauté Aromatics:**
   - In a large pot, heat olive oil over medium heat. Add onion and garlic; sauté until softened.
2. **Cook Mushrooms:**
   - Add mushrooms and cook until browned.
3. **Add Broth and Rice:**
   - Stir in vegetable broth, wild rice, thyme, salt, and pepper. Bring to a boil.
4. **Simmer:**
   - Reduce heat and simmer for 45 minutes or until rice is tender. If using spinach, stir it in during the last 5 minutes.
5. **Serve:**
   - Ladle into bowls and serve hot.

Curried Pumpkin Soup

Ingredients

- 2 tablespoons olive oil
- 1 onion, chopped
- 2 cloves garlic, minced
- 1 tablespoon fresh ginger, minced
- 1 can (15 ounces) pumpkin puree
- 4 cups vegetable broth
- 1 can (13.5 ounces) coconut milk
- 2 tablespoons curry powder
- Salt and pepper to taste
- Optional toppings: pumpkin seeds, fresh cilantro

Instructions

1. **Sauté Aromatics:**
   - In a large pot, heat olive oil over medium heat. Add onion, garlic, and ginger; sauté until onion is translucent.
2. **Add Pumpkin and Broth:**
   - Stir in pumpkin puree, vegetable broth, coconut milk, and curry powder. Bring to a boil.
3. **Simmer:**
   - Reduce heat and let simmer for 15-20 minutes. Season with salt and pepper.
4. **Blend:**
   - Use an immersion blender to puree the soup until smooth.
5. **Serve:**
   - Ladle into bowls and top with pumpkin seeds and fresh cilantro if desired.

Cabbage Roll Soup

Ingredients

- 1 pound ground beef (or turkey)
- 1 onion, chopped
- 2 cloves garlic, minced
- 1 small head of cabbage, chopped
- 1 can (14.5 ounces) diced tomatoes
- 4 cups beef broth
- 1 tablespoon tomato paste
- 1 teaspoon paprika
- Salt and pepper to taste
- Cooked rice (optional, for serving)

Instructions

1. **Brown the Meat:**
    - In a large pot, cook ground beef over medium heat until browned. Drain excess fat.
2. **Sauté Vegetables:**
    - Add onion and garlic; sauté until onion is translucent. Stir in chopped cabbage and cook until slightly softened.
3. **Add Tomatoes and Broth:**
    - Stir in diced tomatoes, beef broth, tomato paste, paprika, salt, and pepper. Bring to a boil.
4. **Simmer:**
    - Reduce heat and let simmer for 30-40 minutes until cabbage is tender.
5. **Serve:**
    - Serve hot, with cooked rice if desired.

Italian Sausage and Kale Soup

Ingredients

- 2 tablespoons olive oil
- 1 pound Italian sausage, casings removed
- 1 onion, chopped
- 3 cloves garlic, minced
- 4 cups chicken broth
- 1 can (14.5 ounces) diced tomatoes
- 4 cups kale, chopped
- 1 cup carrots, diced
- 1 teaspoon Italian seasoning
- Salt and pepper to taste

Instructions

1. **Brown the Sausage:**
   - In a large pot, heat olive oil over medium heat. Add sausage and cook until browned. Break it up into smaller pieces as it cooks.
2. **Sauté Vegetables:**
   - Add onion, garlic, and carrots; sauté until softened.
3. **Add Broth and Kale:**
   - Stir in chicken broth, diced tomatoes, kale, Italian seasoning, salt, and pepper. Bring to a boil.
4. **Simmer:**
   - Reduce heat and let simmer for 20-25 minutes until kale is tender.
5. **Serve:**
   - Ladle into bowls and enjoy hot.

Sausage and Lentil Soup

Ingredients

- 2 tablespoons olive oil
- 1 pound sausage (Italian or smoked), sliced
- 1 onion, chopped
- 2 carrots, diced
- 2 celery stalks, diced
- 3 cloves garlic, minced
- 1 cup lentils, rinsed
- 6 cups vegetable or chicken broth
- 1 teaspoon thyme
- Salt and pepper to taste

Instructions

1. **Sauté Sausage:**
    - In a large pot, heat olive oil over medium heat. Add sausage and cook until browned. Remove and set aside.
2. **Sauté Vegetables:**
    - In the same pot, add onion, carrots, and celery; sauté until softened. Stir in garlic and cook for an additional minute.
3. **Add Lentils and Broth:**
    - Stir in lentils, broth, thyme, salt, and pepper. Bring to a boil.
4. **Simmer:**
    - Reduce heat and let simmer for 30-40 minutes until lentils are tender.
5. **Combine:**
    - Return sausage to the pot, heat through, and serve hot.

Spicy Black Bean Soup

Ingredients

- 2 tablespoons olive oil
- 1 onion, chopped
- 2 cloves garlic, minced
- 1 teaspoon cumin
- 1 teaspoon chili powder
- 2 cans (15 ounces each) black beans, drained and rinsed
- 4 cups vegetable broth
- 1 can (14.5 ounces) diced tomatoes with green chilies
- Salt and pepper to taste
- Optional toppings: sour cream, avocado, cilantro

Instructions

1. **Sauté Aromatics:**
    - In a large pot, heat olive oil over medium heat. Add onion and garlic; sauté until softened. Stir in cumin and chili powder and cook for 1 minute.
2. **Add Beans and Broth:**
    - Stir in black beans, vegetable broth, and diced tomatoes. Bring to a boil.
3. **Simmer:**
    - Reduce heat and let simmer for 20-30 minutes.
4. **Blend (Optional):**
    - For a smoother texture, use an immersion blender to puree part of the soup.
5. **Serve:**
    - Ladle into bowls and top with sour cream, avocado, and cilantro if desired.

Coconut Curry Chicken Soup

Ingredients

- 2 tablespoons coconut oil
- 1 pound chicken breasts, diced
- 1 onion, chopped
- 2 cloves garlic, minced
- 1 tablespoon fresh ginger, minced
- 1 tablespoon curry powder
- 4 cups chicken broth
- 1 can (13.5 ounces) coconut milk
- 2 cups vegetables (carrots, bell peppers, etc.)
- Salt and pepper to taste
- Fresh cilantro for garnish

Instructions

1. **Cook Chicken:**
    - In a large pot, heat coconut oil over medium heat. Add chicken and cook until browned. Remove and set aside.
2. **Sauté Aromatics:**
    - In the same pot, add onion, garlic, and ginger; sauté until softened. Stir in curry powder and cook for 1 minute.
3. **Add Broth and Coconut Milk:**
    - Stir in chicken broth and coconut milk, and bring to a boil. Add vegetables and return chicken to the pot.
4. **Simmer:**
    - Reduce heat and let simmer for 20-25 minutes until chicken is cooked through and vegetables are tender.
5. **Serve:**
    - Garnish with fresh cilantro and serve hot.

Creamy Broccoli Cheddar Soup

Ingredients

- 2 tablespoons butter
- 1 onion, chopped
- 2 cloves garlic, minced
- 4 cups broccoli florets
- 4 cups vegetable or chicken broth
- 1 cup heavy cream
- 2 cups shredded cheddar cheese
- Salt and pepper to taste

Instructions

1. **Sauté Aromatics:**
    - In a large pot, melt butter over medium heat. Add onion and garlic; sauté until softened.
2. **Add Broccoli and Broth:**
    - Stir in broccoli and broth, bringing to a boil. Reduce heat and let simmer until broccoli is tender, about 15 minutes.
3. **Blend:**
    - Use an immersion blender to puree the soup to your desired consistency.
4. **Add Cream and Cheese:**
    - Stir in heavy cream and shredded cheddar cheese until melted. Season with salt and pepper.
5. **Serve:**
    - Ladle into bowls and enjoy hot.

Savory Beef and Potato Soup

Ingredients

- 2 tablespoons olive oil
- 1 pound beef stew meat, cubed
- 1 onion, chopped
- 3 cloves garlic, minced
- 4 cups beef broth
- 2 cups potatoes, diced
- 2 carrots, diced
- 1 teaspoon thyme
- Salt and pepper to taste

Instructions

1. **Brown the Meat:**
    - In a large pot, heat olive oil over medium heat. Add cubed beef and brown on all sides. Remove and set aside.
2. **Sauté Vegetables:**
    - In the same pot, add onion, garlic, carrots, and potatoes; sauté for about 5 minutes.
3. **Add Beef and Broth:**
    - Return beef to the pot and stir in beef broth, thyme, salt, and pepper. Bring to a boil.
4. **Simmer:**
    - Reduce heat and let simmer for about 1.5 hours or until beef is tender and vegetables are cooked.
5. **Serve:**
    - Ladle into bowls and serve hot.

Curried Pumpkin Soup

Ingredients

- 2 tablespoons olive oil
- 1 onion, chopped
- 2 cloves garlic, minced
- 1 tablespoon fresh ginger, minced
- 1 can (15 ounces) pumpkin puree
- 4 cups vegetable broth
- 1 can (13.5 ounces) coconut milk
- 2 tablespoons curry powder
- Salt and pepper to taste
- Optional toppings: pumpkin seeds, fresh cilantro

Instructions

1. **Sauté Aromatics:**
   - In a large pot, heat olive oil over medium heat. Add onion, garlic, and ginger; sauté until onion is translucent.
2. **Add Pumpkin and Broth:**
   - Stir in pumpkin puree, vegetable broth, coconut milk, and curry powder. Bring to a boil.
3. **Simmer:**
   - Reduce heat and let simmer for 15-20 minutes. Season with salt and pepper.
4. **Blend:**
   - Use an immersion blender to puree the soup until smooth.
5. **Serve:**
   - Ladle into bowls and top with pumpkin seeds and fresh cilantro if desired.

Cabbage Roll Soup

Ingredients

- 1 pound ground beef (or turkey)
- 1 onion, chopped
- 2 cloves garlic, minced
- 1 small head of cabbage, chopped
- 1 can (14.5 ounces) diced tomatoes
- 4 cups beef broth
- 1 tablespoon tomato paste
- 1 teaspoon paprika
- Salt and pepper to taste
- Cooked rice (optional, for serving)

Instructions

1. **Brown the Meat:**
   - In a large pot, cook ground beef over medium heat until browned. Drain excess fat.
2. **Sauté Vegetables:**
   - Add onion and garlic; sauté until onion is translucent. Stir in chopped cabbage and cook until slightly softened.
3. **Add Tomatoes and Broth:**
   - Stir in diced tomatoes, beef broth, tomato paste, paprika, salt, and pepper. Bring to a boil.
4. **Simmer:**
   - Reduce heat and let simmer for 30-40 minutes until cabbage is tender.
5. **Serve:**
   - Serve hot, with cooked rice if desired.

Italian Sausage and Kale Soup

Ingredients

- 2 tablespoons olive oil
- 1 pound Italian sausage, casings removed
- 1 onion, chopped
- 3 cloves garlic, minced
- 4 cups chicken broth
- 1 can (14.5 ounces) diced tomatoes
- 4 cups kale, chopped
- 1 cup carrots, diced
- 1 teaspoon Italian seasoning
- Salt and pepper to taste

Instructions

1. **Brown the Sausage:**
   - In a large pot, heat olive oil over medium heat. Add sausage and cook until browned. Break it up into smaller pieces as it cooks.
2. **Sauté Vegetables:**
   - Add onion, garlic, and carrots; sauté until softened.
3. **Add Broth and Kale:**
   - Stir in chicken broth, diced tomatoes, kale, Italian seasoning, salt, and pepper. Bring to a boil.
4. **Simmer:**
   - Reduce heat and let simmer for 20-25 minutes until kale is tender.
5. **Serve:**
   - Ladle into bowls and enjoy hot.

Sausage and Lentil Soup

Ingredients

- 2 tablespoons olive oil
- 1 pound sausage (Italian or smoked), sliced
- 1 onion, chopped
- 2 carrots, diced
- 2 celery stalks, diced
- 3 cloves garlic, minced
- 1 cup lentils, rinsed
- 6 cups vegetable or chicken broth
- 1 teaspoon thyme
- Salt and pepper to taste

Instructions

1. **Sauté Sausage:**
    - In a large pot, heat olive oil over medium heat. Add sausage and cook until browned. Remove and set aside.
2. **Sauté Vegetables:**
    - In the same pot, add onion, carrots, and celery; sauté until softened. Stir in garlic and cook for an additional minute.
3. **Add Lentils and Broth:**
    - Stir in lentils, broth, thyme, salt, and pepper. Bring to a boil.
4. **Simmer:**
    - Reduce heat and let simmer for 30-40 minutes until lentils are tender.
5. **Combine:**
    - Return sausage to the pot, heat through, and serve hot.

Spicy Black Bean Soup

Ingredients

- 2 tablespoons olive oil
- 1 onion, chopped
- 2 cloves garlic, minced
- 1 teaspoon cumin
- 1 teaspoon chili powder
- 2 cans (15 ounces each) black beans, drained and rinsed
- 4 cups vegetable broth
- 1 can (14.5 ounces) diced tomatoes with green chilies
- Salt and pepper to taste
- Optional toppings: sour cream, avocado, cilantro

Instructions

1. **Sauté Aromatics:**
   - In a large pot, heat olive oil over medium heat. Add onion and garlic; sauté until softened. Stir in cumin and chili powder and cook for 1 minute.
2. **Add Beans and Broth:**
   - Stir in black beans, vegetable broth, and diced tomatoes. Bring to a boil.
3. **Simmer:**
   - Reduce heat and let simmer for 20-30 minutes.
4. **Blend (Optional):**
   - For a smoother texture, use an immersion blender to puree part of the soup.
5. **Serve:**
   - Ladle into bowls and top with sour cream, avocado, and cilantro if desired.

Coconut Curry Chicken Soup

Ingredients

- 2 tablespoons coconut oil
- 1 pound chicken breasts, diced
- 1 onion, chopped
- 2 cloves garlic, minced
- 1 tablespoon fresh ginger, minced
- 1 tablespoon curry powder
- 4 cups chicken broth
- 1 can (13.5 ounces) coconut milk
- 2 cups vegetables (carrots, bell peppers, etc.)
- Salt and pepper to taste
- Fresh cilantro for garnish

Instructions

1. **Cook Chicken:**
    - In a large pot, heat coconut oil over medium heat. Add chicken and cook until browned. Remove and set aside.
2. **Sauté Aromatics:**
    - In the same pot, add onion, garlic, and ginger; sauté until softened. Stir in curry powder and cook for 1 minute.
3. **Add Broth and Coconut Milk:**
    - Stir in chicken broth and coconut milk, and bring to a boil. Add vegetables and return chicken to the pot.
4. **Simmer:**
    - Reduce heat and let simmer for 20-25 minutes until chicken is cooked through and vegetables are tender.
5. **Serve:**
    - Garnish with fresh cilantro and serve hot.

Creamy Broccoli Cheddar Soup

Ingredients

- 2 tablespoons butter
- 1 onion, chopped
- 2 cloves garlic, minced
- 4 cups broccoli florets
- 4 cups vegetable or chicken broth
- 1 cup heavy cream
- 2 cups shredded cheddar cheese
- Salt and pepper to taste

Instructions

1. **Sauté Aromatics:**
    - In a large pot, melt butter over medium heat. Add onion and garlic; sauté until softened.
2. **Add Broccoli and Broth:**
    - Stir in broccoli and broth, bringing to a boil. Reduce heat and let simmer until broccoli is tender, about 15 minutes.
3. **Blend:**
    - Use an immersion blender to puree the soup to your desired consistency.
4. **Add Cream and Cheese:**
    - Stir in heavy cream and shredded cheddar cheese until melted. Season with salt and pepper.
5. **Serve:**
    - Ladle into bowls and enjoy hot.

Savory Beef and Potato Soup

Ingredients

- 2 tablespoons olive oil
- 1 pound beef stew meat, cubed
- 1 onion, chopped
- 3 cloves garlic, minced
- 4 cups beef broth
- 2 cups potatoes, diced
- 2 carrots, diced
- 1 teaspoon thyme
- Salt and pepper to taste

Instructions

1. **Brown the Meat:**
   - In a large pot, heat olive oil over medium heat. Add cubed beef and brown on all sides. Remove and set aside.
2. **Sauté Vegetables:**
   - In the same pot, add onion, garlic, carrots, and potatoes; sauté for about 5 minutes.
3. **Add Beef and Broth:**
   - Return beef to the pot and stir in beef broth, thyme, salt, and pepper. Bring to a boil.
4. **Simmer:**
   - Reduce heat and let simmer for about 1.5 hours or until beef is tender and vegetables are cooked.
5. **Serve:**
   - Ladle into bowls and serve hot.

Shrimp and Corn Chowder

Ingredients

- 2 tablespoons butter
- 1 onion, chopped
- 2 cloves garlic, minced
- 2 cups corn (fresh or frozen)
- 4 cups seafood stock (or chicken broth)
- 1 cup diced potatoes
- 1 pound shrimp, peeled and deveined
- 1 cup heavy cream
- Salt and pepper to taste
- Chopped fresh parsley for garnish

Instructions

1. **Sauté Aromatics:**
   - In a large pot, melt butter over medium heat. Add onion and garlic; sauté until onion is translucent.
2. **Add Corn and Potatoes:**
   - Stir in corn and diced potatoes. Cook for a few minutes.
3. **Add Stock:**
   - Pour in seafood stock, bring to a boil, then reduce heat and simmer until potatoes are tender, about 15 minutes.
4. **Add Shrimp:**
   - Add shrimp to the pot and cook until they turn pink, about 3-5 minutes.
5. **Finish with Cream:**
   - Stir in heavy cream, season with salt and pepper. Heat through and serve hot, garnished with fresh parsley.

Chicken and Wild Rice Soup

Ingredients

- 2 tablespoons olive oil
- 1 onion, chopped
- 2 carrots, diced
- 2 celery stalks, diced
- 3 cloves garlic, minced
- 1 cup wild rice, rinsed
- 8 cups chicken broth
- 2 cups cooked chicken, shredded
- 1 cup heavy cream
- Salt and pepper to taste
- Fresh thyme for garnish

Instructions

1. **Sauté Vegetables:**
    - In a large pot, heat olive oil over medium heat. Add onion, carrots, and celery; sauté until softened.
2. **Add Garlic and Rice:**
    - Stir in garlic and wild rice, cooking for another minute.
3. **Add Broth:**
    - Pour in chicken broth and bring to a boil. Reduce heat and simmer for 30-40 minutes until rice is tender.
4. **Add Chicken and Cream:**
    - Stir in shredded chicken and heavy cream. Season with salt and pepper.
5. **Serve:**
    - Garnish with fresh thyme and serve hot.

Sweet Potato and Black Bean Soup

Ingredients

- 2 tablespoons olive oil
- 1 onion, chopped
- 2 cloves garlic, minced
- 1 teaspoon cumin
- 4 cups sweet potatoes, peeled and diced
- 4 cups vegetable broth
- 1 can (15 ounces) black beans, drained and rinsed
- Salt and pepper to taste
- Optional toppings: avocado, cilantro, lime juice

Instructions

1. **Sauté Aromatics:**
    - In a large pot, heat olive oil over medium heat. Add onion and garlic; sauté until softened. Stir in cumin and cook for 1 minute.
2. **Add Sweet Potatoes and Broth:**
    - Stir in sweet potatoes and vegetable broth. Bring to a boil, then reduce heat and simmer for 20 minutes until sweet potatoes are tender.
3. **Add Black Beans:**
    - Stir in black beans and heat through. Season with salt and pepper.
4. **Blend (Optional):**
    - For a smoother texture, use an immersion blender to puree part of the soup.
5. **Serve:**
    - Ladle into bowls and top with avocado, cilantro, and lime juice if desired.

Mediterranean Chickpea Soup

Ingredients

- 2 tablespoons olive oil
- 1 onion, chopped
- 2 cloves garlic, minced
- 1 teaspoon cumin
- 1 teaspoon smoked paprika
- 4 cups vegetable broth
- 1 can (15 ounces) chickpeas, drained and rinsed
- 1 can (14.5 ounces) diced tomatoes
- 2 cups spinach or kale
- Salt and pepper to taste
- Fresh lemon juice for serving

Instructions

1. **Sauté Aromatics:**
   - In a large pot, heat olive oil over medium heat. Add onion and garlic; sauté until softened. Stir in cumin and smoked paprika.
2. **Add Broth and Chickpeas:**
   - Pour in vegetable broth, chickpeas, and diced tomatoes. Bring to a boil, then reduce heat and simmer for 15 minutes.
3. **Add Greens:**
   - Stir in spinach or kale and cook until wilted. Season with salt and pepper.
4. **Serve:**
   - Ladle into bowls and drizzle with fresh lemon juice.

Borscht (Beet Soup)

Ingredients

- 2 tablespoons vegetable oil
- 1 onion, chopped
- 2 carrots, grated
- 2 cloves garlic, minced
- 4 cups vegetable broth
- 3 medium beets, peeled and grated
- 1 potato, diced
- 1 tablespoon vinegar
- Salt and pepper to taste
- Sour cream and fresh dill for serving

Instructions

1. **Sauté Vegetables:**
    - In a large pot, heat vegetable oil over medium heat. Add onion and carrots; sauté until softened. Stir in garlic and cook for another minute.
2. **Add Broth and Beets:**
    - Pour in vegetable broth, grated beets, and diced potato. Bring to a boil, then reduce heat and simmer for about 30 minutes until beets and potatoes are tender.
3. **Finish the Soup:**
    - Stir in vinegar and season with salt and pepper.
4. **Serve:**
    - Ladle into bowls and serve with a dollop of sour cream and fresh dill.

Pho (Vietnamese Noodle Soup)

Ingredients

- 8 cups beef broth
- 1 onion, halved
- 2 cloves garlic, smashed
- 1 piece ginger (2 inches), sliced
- 2 star anise
- 1 cinnamon stick
- 1 pound beef (flank or sirloin), thinly sliced
- 8 ounces rice noodles
- Fresh herbs (basil, cilantro, mint)
- Lime wedges
- Bean sprouts and jalapeños for garnish

Instructions

1. **Make Broth:**
   - In a large pot, combine beef broth, onion, garlic, ginger, star anise, and cinnamon stick. Bring to a simmer and let cook for 30 minutes.
2. **Prepare Noodles:**
   - Cook rice noodles according to package instructions. Drain and set aside.
3. **Add Beef:**
   - Remove the aromatics from the broth and bring it back to a boil. Add thinly sliced beef to the broth and cook until just done, about 2-3 minutes.
4. **Assemble Bowls:**
   - In bowls, add cooked rice noodles and top with beef. Ladle hot broth over the top.
5. **Serve:**
   - Garnish with fresh herbs, lime wedges, bean sprouts, and jalapeños.

Chicken and Dumpling Soup

Ingredients

- 2 tablespoons butter
- 1 onion, chopped
- 2 carrots, diced
- 2 celery stalks, diced
- 3 cloves garlic, minced
- 6 cups chicken broth
- 2 cups cooked chicken, shredded
- 1 teaspoon thyme
- Salt and pepper to taste
- **Dumplings:**
    - 2 cups all-purpose flour
    - 1 tablespoon baking powder
    - 1 teaspoon salt
    - 3/4 cup milk
    - 1/4 cup butter, melted

Instructions

1. **Sauté Vegetables:**
    - In a large pot, melt butter over medium heat. Add onion, carrots, and celery; sauté until softened. Stir in garlic and cook for 1 minute.
2. **Add Broth and Chicken:**
    - Pour in chicken broth, add shredded chicken, thyme, salt, and pepper. Bring to a boil.
3. **Make Dumpling Batter:**
    - In a bowl, mix flour, baking powder, and salt. Stir in milk and melted butter until just combined.
4. **Cook Dumplings:**
    - Drop spoonfuls of dumpling batter into the boiling soup. Cover and simmer for 15-20 minutes until dumplings are cooked through.
5. **Serve:**
    - Ladle into bowls and enjoy hot.

Egg Drop Soup

Ingredients

- 4 cups chicken broth
- 2 eggs, lightly beaten
- 1 tablespoon cornstarch mixed with 2 tablespoons water (optional for thickening)
- 2 green onions, chopped
- Salt and pepper to taste
- Soy sauce for serving

Instructions

1. **Heat Broth:**
    - In a pot, bring chicken broth to a boil.
2. **Add Cornstarch (Optional):**
    - If thickening, stir in cornstarch mixture and simmer for a minute.
3. **Add Eggs:**
    - Slowly drizzle in beaten eggs while stirring the broth gently to create ribbons.
4. **Finish:**
    - Stir in green onions and season with salt and pepper.
5. **Serve:**
    - Ladle into bowls and drizzle with soy sauce if desired.

Roasted Garlic and Cauliflower Soup

Ingredients

- 1 head cauliflower, chopped
- 1 bulb garlic, roasted
- 2 tablespoons olive oil
- 1 onion, chopped
- 4 cups vegetable broth
- 1 cup heavy cream (or coconut milk)
- Salt and pepper to taste
- Fresh chives for garnish

Instructions

1. **Roast Cauliflower and Garlic:**
    - Preheat oven to 400°F (200°C). Toss cauliflower with olive oil, salt, and pepper. Roast on a baking sheet for 25-30 minutes until golden. Squeeze roasted garlic from its skin.
2. **Sauté Onion:**
    - In a pot, sauté onion until soft. Add roasted cauliflower and garlic.
3. **Add Broth:**
    - Pour in vegetable broth and simmer for 10 minutes.
4. **Blend:**
    - Use an immersion blender to puree the soup until smooth. Stir in heavy cream and heat through.
5. **Serve:**
    - Garnish with fresh chives and serve hot.

Kale and Quinoa Soup

Ingredients

- 2 tablespoons olive oil
- 1 onion, chopped
- 2 carrots, diced
- 2 cloves garlic, minced
- 1 teaspoon dried thyme
- 6 cups vegetable broth
- 1 cup quinoa, rinsed
- 4 cups chopped kale
- Salt and pepper to taste
- Juice of 1 lemon

Instructions

1. **Sauté Vegetables:**
    - In a large pot, heat olive oil over medium heat. Add onion and carrots; sauté until softened.
2. **Add Garlic and Thyme:**
    - Stir in garlic and thyme; cook for 1 minute.
3. **Add Broth and Quinoa:**
    - Pour in vegetable broth and bring to a boil. Stir in quinoa and simmer for 15 minutes.
4. **Add Kale:**
    - Stir in kale and cook until wilted, about 5 minutes. Season with salt and pepper and stir in lemon juice.
5. **Serve:**
    - Ladle into bowls and enjoy hot.

Seafood Gumbo

Ingredients

- 2 tablespoons vegetable oil
- 1/2 cup flour
- 1 onion, chopped
- 1 bell pepper, diced
- 2 celery stalks, diced
- 3 cloves garlic, minced
- 6 cups seafood stock
- 1 can (14.5 ounces) diced tomatoes
- 1 pound shrimp, peeled and deveined
- 1 pound crab meat
- 1 tablespoon Cajun seasoning
- 2 cups okra, sliced
- Salt and pepper to taste
- Cooked rice for serving
- Chopped green onions for garnish

Instructions

1. **Make Roux:**
   - In a large pot, heat oil over medium heat. Gradually whisk in flour and cook, stirring constantly, until brown, about 15-20 minutes.
2. **Add Vegetables:**
   - Add onion, bell pepper, celery, and garlic; sauté until softened.
3. **Add Stock and Tomatoes:**
   - Stir in seafood stock and diced tomatoes. Bring to a simmer.
4. **Add Seafood and Seasoning:**
   - Add shrimp, crab meat, Cajun seasoning, and okra. Simmer for 15-20 minutes until seafood is cooked through. Season with salt and pepper.
5. **Serve:**
   - Serve over cooked rice and garnish with green onions.

Spicy Thai Soup (Tom Yum)

Ingredients

- 4 cups chicken or vegetable broth
- 1 stalk lemongrass, chopped
- 3-4 slices galangal (or ginger)
- 3-4 kaffir lime leaves
- 2-3 Thai bird chilies, smashed
- 200g mushrooms, sliced
- 300g shrimp, peeled and deveined
- 2 tablespoons fish sauce
- Juice of 1 lime
- Fresh cilantro for garnish

Instructions

1. **Prepare Broth:**
    - In a pot, bring broth to a boil. Add lemongrass, galangal, lime leaves, and chilies. Simmer for 10 minutes.
2. **Add Mushrooms:**
    - Stir in mushrooms and cook for another 5 minutes.
3. **Add Shrimp and Seasoning:**
    - Add shrimp and cook until they turn pink. Stir in fish sauce and lime juice.
4. **Serve:**
    - Remove from heat and garnish with fresh cilantro. Serve hot.

Ham and Bean Soup

Ingredients

- 1 tablespoon olive oil
- 1 onion, chopped
- 2 carrots, diced
- 2 celery stalks, diced
- 3 cloves garlic, minced
- 1 pound ham, diced
- 6 cups chicken broth
- 1 can (15 ounces) white beans, drained and rinsed
- 1 teaspoon thyme
- Salt and pepper to taste
- Chopped parsley for garnish

Instructions

1. **Sauté Vegetables:**
   - In a large pot, heat olive oil over medium heat. Add onion, carrots, and celery; sauté until softened.
2. **Add Garlic and Ham:**
   - Stir in garlic and ham; cook for another 2-3 minutes.
3. **Add Broth and Beans:**
   - Pour in chicken broth and add white beans. Bring to a boil, then reduce heat and simmer for 20-30 minutes.
4. **Season:**
   - Stir in thyme, salt, and pepper. Adjust seasoning as needed.
5. **Serve:**
   - Ladle into bowls and garnish with chopped parsley.

Pasta Fagioli

Ingredients

- 2 tablespoons olive oil
- 1 onion, chopped
- 2 carrots, diced
- 2 celery stalks, diced
- 3 cloves garlic, minced
- 6 cups vegetable broth
- 1 can (15 ounces) cannellini beans, drained and rinsed
- 1 cup small pasta (ditalini or elbow)
- 1 teaspoon Italian seasoning
- Salt and pepper to taste
- Fresh parsley for garnish

Instructions

1. **Sauté Vegetables:**
    - In a large pot, heat olive oil over medium heat. Add onion, carrots, and celery; sauté until softened.
2. **Add Garlic:**
    - Stir in garlic and cook for 1 minute.
3. **Add Broth and Beans:**
    - Pour in vegetable broth and add cannellini beans. Bring to a boil.
4. **Add Pasta and Seasoning:**
    - Stir in pasta and Italian seasoning. Cook until pasta is tender, about 10-12 minutes.
5. **Serve:**
    - Season with salt and pepper. Ladle into bowls and garnish with fresh parsley.

Zucchini and Tomato Soup

Ingredients

- 2 tablespoons olive oil
- 1 onion, chopped
- 2 cloves garlic, minced
- 4 cups zucchini, diced
- 4 cups diced tomatoes (canned or fresh)
- 4 cups vegetable broth
- 1 teaspoon basil
- Salt and pepper to taste
- Fresh basil for garnish

Instructions

1. **Sauté Onion and Garlic:**
    - In a large pot, heat olive oil over medium heat. Add onion and sauté until softened. Stir in garlic and cook for 1 minute.
2. **Add Zucchini and Tomatoes:**
    - Add zucchini and diced tomatoes; cook for about 5 minutes.
3. **Add Broth and Seasoning:**
    - Pour in vegetable broth and add basil. Bring to a boil, then reduce heat and simmer for 15 minutes.
4. **Blend (Optional):**
    - For a smoother texture, use an immersion blender to puree the soup.
5. **Serve:**
    - Season with salt and pepper and garnish with fresh basil.

Chicken Pho

Ingredients

- 8 cups chicken broth
- 1 onion, halved
- 1 ginger root (2 inches), sliced
- 2 star anise
- 1 cinnamon stick
- 1 pound chicken (thighs or breast)
- 8 ounces rice noodles
- Fresh herbs (basil, cilantro, mint)
- Lime wedges
- Bean sprouts and jalapeños for garnish

Instructions

1. **Prepare Broth:**
   - In a pot, combine chicken broth, onion, ginger, star anise, and cinnamon stick. Bring to a simmer and cook for 30 minutes.
2. **Cook Chicken:**
   - Remove onion and spices. Add chicken to the broth and cook until fully cooked, about 15 minutes. Remove chicken, shred it, and set aside.
3. **Prepare Noodles:**
   - Cook rice noodles according to package instructions. Drain and set aside.
4. **Assemble Bowls:**
   - In bowls, add cooked noodles and top with shredded chicken. Ladle hot broth over the top.
5. **Serve:**
   - Garnish with fresh herbs, lime wedges, bean sprouts, and jalapeños.

Spaghetti and Meatball Soup

Ingredients

- 2 tablespoons olive oil
- 1 onion, chopped
- 2 cloves garlic, minced
- 6 cups chicken or vegetable broth
- 1 can (14.5 ounces) diced tomatoes
- 1 pound meatballs (homemade or store-bought)
- 1 cup spaghetti, broken into pieces
- 1 teaspoon Italian seasoning
- Salt and pepper to taste
- Grated Parmesan for serving

Instructions

1. **Sauté Onion and Garlic:**
    - In a large pot, heat olive oil over medium heat. Add onion and sauté until softened. Stir in garlic and cook for 1 minute.
2. **Add Broth and Tomatoes:**
    - Pour in broth and add diced tomatoes. Bring to a boil.
3. **Add Meatballs and Spaghetti:**
    - Add meatballs and broken spaghetti. Cook until spaghetti is tender and meatballs are heated through, about 10 minutes.
4. **Season:**
    - Stir in Italian seasoning, salt, and pepper.
5. **Serve:**
    - Ladle into bowls and sprinkle with grated Parmesan.

Vegetable and Barley Soup

Ingredients

- 2 tablespoons olive oil
- 1 onion, chopped
- 2 carrots, diced
- 2 celery stalks, diced
- 3 cloves garlic, minced
- 6 cups vegetable broth
- 1 cup barley
- 2 cups mixed vegetables (e.g., green beans, corn, peas)
- 1 teaspoon thyme
- Salt and pepper to taste
- Chopped parsley for garnish

Instructions

1. **Sauté Vegetables:**
    - In a large pot, heat olive oil over medium heat. Add onion, carrots, and celery; sauté until softened.
2. **Add Garlic and Broth:**
    - Stir in garlic and cook for 1 minute. Pour in vegetable broth and bring to a boil.
3. **Add Barley:**
    - Add barley and reduce heat to a simmer. Cook for 30 minutes.
4. **Add Mixed Vegetables:**
    - Stir in mixed vegetables and thyme. Cook until heated through, about 10 minutes. Season with salt and pepper.
5. **Serve:**
    - Ladle into bowls and garnish with chopped parsley.

Kale and Quinoa Soup

Ingredients

- 2 tablespoons olive oil
- 1 onion, chopped
- 2 carrots, diced
- 2 cloves garlic, minced
- 1 teaspoon dried thyme
- 6 cups vegetable broth
- 1 cup quinoa, rinsed
- 4 cups chopped kale
- Salt and pepper to taste
- Juice of 1 lemon

Instructions

1. **Sauté Vegetables:**
    - In a large pot, heat olive oil over medium heat. Add onion and carrots; sauté until softened.
2. **Add Garlic and Thyme:**
    - Stir in garlic and thyme; cook for 1 minute.
3. **Add Broth and Quinoa:**
    - Pour in vegetable broth and bring to a boil. Stir in quinoa and simmer for 15 minutes.
4. **Add Kale:**
    - Stir in kale and cook until wilted, about 5 minutes. Season with salt and pepper and stir in lemon juice.
5. **Serve:**
    - Ladle into bowls and enjoy hot.

Seafood Gumbo

Ingredients

- 2 tablespoons vegetable oil
- 1/2 cup flour
- 1 onion, chopped
- 1 bell pepper, diced
- 2 celery stalks, diced
- 3 cloves garlic, minced
- 6 cups seafood stock
- 1 can (14.5 ounces) diced tomatoes
- 1 pound shrimp, peeled and deveined
- 1 pound crab meat
- 1 tablespoon Cajun seasoning
- 2 cups okra, sliced
- Salt and pepper to taste
- Cooked rice for serving
- Chopped green onions for garnish

Instructions

1. **Make Roux:**
    - In a large pot, heat oil over medium heat. Gradually whisk in flour and cook, stirring constantly, until brown, about 15-20 minutes.
2. **Add Vegetables:**
    - Add onion, bell pepper, celery, and garlic; sauté until softened.
3. **Add Stock and Tomatoes:**
    - Stir in seafood stock and diced tomatoes. Bring to a simmer.
4. **Add Seafood and Seasoning:**
    - Add shrimp, crab meat, Cajun seasoning, and okra. Simmer for 15-20 minutes until seafood is cooked through. Season with salt and pepper.
5. **Serve:**
    - Serve over cooked rice and garnish with green onions.

Spicy Thai Soup (Tom Yum)

Ingredients

- 4 cups chicken or vegetable broth
- 1 stalk lemongrass, chopped
- 3-4 slices galangal (or ginger)
- 3-4 kaffir lime leaves
- 2-3 Thai bird chilies, smashed
- 200g mushrooms, sliced
- 300g shrimp, peeled and deveined
- 2 tablespoons fish sauce
- Juice of 1 lime
- Fresh cilantro for garnish

Instructions

1. **Prepare Broth:**
    - In a pot, bring broth to a boil. Add lemongrass, galangal, lime leaves, and chilies. Simmer for 10 minutes.
2. **Add Mushrooms:**
    - Stir in mushrooms and cook for another 5 minutes.
3. **Add Shrimp and Seasoning:**
    - Add shrimp and cook until they turn pink. Stir in fish sauce and lime juice.
4. **Serve:**
    - Remove from heat and garnish with fresh cilantro. Serve hot.

Ham and Bean Soup

Ingredients

- 1 tablespoon olive oil
- 1 onion, chopped
- 2 carrots, diced
- 2 celery stalks, diced
- 3 cloves garlic, minced
- 1 pound ham, diced
- 6 cups chicken broth
- 1 can (15 ounces) white beans, drained and rinsed
- 1 teaspoon thyme
- Salt and pepper to taste
- Chopped parsley for garnish

Instructions

1. **Sauté Vegetables:**
   - In a large pot, heat olive oil over medium heat. Add onion, carrots, and celery; sauté until softened.
2. **Add Garlic and Ham:**
   - Stir in garlic and ham; cook for another 2-3 minutes.
3. **Add Broth and Beans:**
   - Pour in chicken broth and add white beans. Bring to a boil, then reduce heat and simmer for 20-30 minutes.
4. **Season:**
   - Stir in thyme, salt, and pepper. Adjust seasoning as needed.
5. **Serve:**
   - Ladle into bowls and garnish with chopped parsley.

Pasta Fagioli

Ingredients

- 2 tablespoons olive oil
- 1 onion, chopped
- 2 carrots, diced
- 2 celery stalks, diced
- 3 cloves garlic, minced
- 6 cups vegetable broth
- 1 can (15 ounces) cannellini beans, drained and rinsed
- 1 cup small pasta (ditalini or elbow)
- 1 teaspoon Italian seasoning
- Salt and pepper to taste
- Fresh parsley for garnish

Instructions

1. **Sauté Vegetables:**
    - In a large pot, heat olive oil over medium heat. Add onion, carrots, and celery; sauté until softened.
2. **Add Garlic:**
    - Stir in garlic and cook for 1 minute.
3. **Add Broth and Beans:**
    - Pour in vegetable broth and add cannellini beans. Bring to a boil.
4. **Add Pasta and Seasoning:**
    - Stir in pasta and Italian seasoning. Cook until pasta is tender, about 10-12 minutes.
5. **Serve:**
    - Season with salt and pepper. Ladle into bowls and garnish with fresh parsley.

Zucchini and Tomato Soup

Ingredients

- 2 tablespoons olive oil
- 1 onion, chopped
- 2 cloves garlic, minced
- 4 cups zucchini, diced
- 4 cups diced tomatoes (canned or fresh)
- 4 cups vegetable broth
- 1 teaspoon basil
- Salt and pepper to taste
- Fresh basil for garnish

Instructions

1. **Sauté Onion and Garlic:**
   - In a large pot, heat olive oil over medium heat. Add onion and sauté until softened. Stir in garlic and cook for 1 minute.
2. **Add Zucchini and Tomatoes:**
   - Add zucchini and diced tomatoes; cook for about 5 minutes.
3. **Add Broth and Seasoning:**
   - Pour in vegetable broth and add basil. Bring to a boil, then reduce heat and simmer for 15 minutes.
4. **Blend (Optional):**
   - For a smoother texture, use an immersion blender to puree the soup.
5. **Serve:**
   - Season with salt and pepper and garnish with fresh basil.

Chicken Pho

Ingredients

- 8 cups chicken broth
- 1 onion, halved
- 1 ginger root (2 inches), sliced
- 2 star anise
- 1 cinnamon stick
- 1 pound chicken (thighs or breast)
- 8 ounces rice noodles
- Fresh herbs (basil, cilantro, mint)
- Lime wedges
- Bean sprouts and jalapeños for garnish

Instructions

1. **Prepare Broth:**
    - In a pot, combine chicken broth, onion, ginger, star anise, and cinnamon stick. Bring to a simmer and cook for 30 minutes.
2. **Cook Chicken:**
    - Remove onion and spices. Add chicken to the broth and cook until fully cooked, about 15 minutes. Remove chicken, shred it, and set aside.
3. **Prepare Noodles:**
    - Cook rice noodles according to package instructions. Drain and set aside.
4. **Assemble Bowls:**
    - In bowls, add cooked noodles and top with shredded chicken. Ladle hot broth over the top.
5. **Serve:**
    - Garnish with fresh herbs, lime wedges, bean sprouts, and jalapeños.

Spaghetti and Meatball Soup

Ingredients

- 2 tablespoons olive oil
- 1 onion, chopped
- 2 cloves garlic, minced
- 6 cups chicken or vegetable broth
- 1 can (14.5 ounces) diced tomatoes
- 1 pound meatballs (homemade or store-bought)
- 1 cup spaghetti, broken into pieces
- 1 teaspoon Italian seasoning
- Salt and pepper to taste
- Grated Parmesan for serving

Instructions

1. **Sauté Onion and Garlic:**
    - In a large pot, heat olive oil over medium heat. Add onion and sauté until softened. Stir in garlic and cook for 1 minute.
2. **Add Broth and Tomatoes:**
    - Pour in broth and add diced tomatoes. Bring to a boil.
3. **Add Meatballs and Spaghetti:**
    - Add meatballs and broken spaghetti. Cook until spaghetti is tender and meatballs are heated through, about 10 minutes.
4. **Season:**
    - Stir in Italian seasoning, salt, and pepper.
5. **Serve:**
    - Ladle into bowls and sprinkle with grated Parmesan.

Vegetable and Barley Soup

Ingredients

- 2 tablespoons olive oil
- 1 onion, chopped
- 2 carrots, diced
- 2 celery stalks, diced
- 3 cloves garlic, minced
- 6 cups vegetable broth
- 1 cup barley
- 2 cups mixed vegetables (e.g., green beans, corn, peas)
- 1 teaspoon thyme
- Salt and pepper to taste
- Chopped parsley for garnish

Instructions

1. **Sauté Vegetables:**
    - In a large pot, heat olive oil over medium heat. Add onion, carrots, and celery; sauté until softened.
2. **Add Garlic and Broth:**
    - Stir in garlic and cook for 1 minute. Pour in vegetable broth and bring to a boil.
3. **Add Barley:**
    - Add barley and reduce heat to a simmer. Cook for 30 minutes.
4. **Add Mixed Vegetables:**
    - Stir in mixed vegetables and thyme. Cook until heated through, about 10 minutes. Season with salt and pepper.
5. **Serve:**
    - Ladle into bowls and garnish with chopped parsley.

Beef and Cabbage Soup

Ingredients

- 2 tablespoons olive oil
- 1 pound ground beef
- 1 onion, chopped
- 2 carrots, diced
- 2 cloves garlic, minced
- 6 cups beef broth
- 1 small head cabbage, chopped
- 1 can (14.5 ounces) diced tomatoes
- 1 teaspoon thyme
- Salt and pepper to taste
- Fresh parsley for garnish

Instructions

1. **Cook Beef:**
    - In a large pot, heat olive oil over medium heat. Add ground beef and cook until browned. Drain excess fat.
2. **Add Vegetables:**
    - Add onion, carrots, and garlic; sauté until softened, about 5 minutes.
3. **Add Broth and Cabbage:**
    - Pour in beef broth and add chopped cabbage. Bring to a boil.
4. **Add Tomatoes and Seasoning:**
    - Stir in diced tomatoes and thyme. Reduce heat and simmer for 30 minutes. Season with salt and pepper.
5. **Serve:**
    - Ladle into bowls and garnish with fresh parsley.

Cheesy Potato Soup

Ingredients

- 4 cups diced potatoes
- 1 onion, chopped
- 2 cloves garlic, minced
- 4 cups chicken or vegetable broth
- 1 cup shredded cheddar cheese
- 1 cup milk
- Salt and pepper to taste
- Chopped green onions for garnish

Instructions

1. **Sauté Onion and Garlic:**
   - In a large pot, sauté onion and garlic in a little oil until softened.
2. **Add Potatoes and Broth:**
   - Add diced potatoes and broth. Bring to a boil, then reduce heat and simmer until potatoes are tender, about 15-20 minutes.
3. **Blend (Optional):**
   - For a smoother texture, use an immersion blender to puree some of the potatoes while leaving some chunks.
4. **Add Cheese and Milk:**
   - Stir in cheese and milk. Cook until cheese is melted and soup is heated through. Season with salt and pepper.
5. **Serve:**
   - Ladle into bowls and garnish with chopped green onions.

Lemon Chicken Orzo Soup

Ingredients

- 1 tablespoon olive oil
- 1 onion, chopped
- 2 carrots, diced
- 2 celery stalks, diced
- 3 cloves garlic, minced
- 6 cups chicken broth
- 1 cup cooked chicken, shredded
- 1 cup orzo pasta
- Juice and zest of 1 lemon
- Fresh parsley for garnish
- Salt and pepper to taste

Instructions

1. **Sauté Vegetables:**
    - In a large pot, heat olive oil over medium heat. Add onion, carrots, and celery; sauté until softened.
2. **Add Garlic:**
    - Stir in garlic and cook for 1 minute.
3. **Add Broth and Chicken:**
    - Pour in chicken broth and bring to a boil. Add shredded chicken.
4. **Add Orzo and Seasoning:**
    - Stir in orzo and cook until tender, about 8-10 minutes. Add lemon juice and zest, and season with salt and pepper.
5. **Serve:**
    - Ladle into bowls and garnish with fresh parsley.

Carrot Ginger Soup

Ingredients

- 2 tablespoons olive oil
- 1 onion, chopped
- 1 pound carrots, peeled and diced
- 2 cloves garlic, minced
- 1 inch ginger, grated
- 4 cups vegetable broth
- 1 teaspoon cumin
- Salt and pepper to taste
- Fresh cilantro for garnish

Instructions

1. **Sauté Vegetables:**
    - In a large pot, heat olive oil over medium heat. Add onion and sauté until softened.
2. **Add Carrots, Garlic, and Ginger:**
    - Stir in carrots, garlic, and ginger; cook for 5 minutes.
3. **Add Broth and Seasoning:**
    - Pour in vegetable broth and cumin. Bring to a boil, then reduce heat and simmer until carrots are tender, about 20 minutes.
4. **Blend:**
    - Use an immersion blender to puree the soup until smooth. Season with salt and pepper.
5. **Serve:**
    - Ladle into bowls and garnish with fresh cilantro.

Tuscan Kale and Sausage Soup

Ingredients

- 2 tablespoons olive oil
- 1 pound Italian sausage, casings removed
- 1 onion, chopped
- 2 cloves garlic, minced
- 6 cups chicken broth
- 2 cups kale, chopped
- 1 can (14.5 ounces) diced tomatoes
- 1 teaspoon Italian seasoning
- Salt and pepper to taste

Instructions

1. **Cook Sausage:**
   - In a large pot, heat olive oil over medium heat. Add sausage and cook until browned.
2. **Add Onion and Garlic:**
   - Stir in onion and garlic; cook until softened.
3. **Add Broth and Kale:**
   - Pour in chicken broth and bring to a simmer. Add chopped kale and cook until wilted.
4. **Add Tomatoes and Seasoning:**
   - Stir in diced tomatoes and Italian seasoning. Season with salt and pepper.
5. **Serve:**
   - Ladle into bowls and enjoy hot.

Stuffed Pepper Soup

Ingredients

- 2 tablespoons olive oil
- 1 onion, chopped
- 2 cloves garlic, minced
- 1 pound ground beef or turkey
- 2 bell peppers, diced
- 1 can (14.5 ounces) diced tomatoes
- 4 cups beef or vegetable broth
- 1 cup cooked rice
- 1 teaspoon Italian seasoning
- Salt and pepper to taste

Instructions

1. **Cook Meat:**
    - In a large pot, heat olive oil over medium heat. Add onion and garlic; sauté until softened. Add ground beef or turkey and cook until browned.
2. **Add Peppers:**
    - Stir in diced bell peppers and cook for about 5 minutes.
3. **Add Tomatoes and Broth:**
    - Pour in diced tomatoes and broth. Bring to a boil.
4. **Add Rice and Seasoning:**
    - Stir in cooked rice and Italian seasoning. Season with salt and pepper. Simmer for 10 minutes.
5. **Serve:**
    - Ladle into bowls and enjoy hot.

Lentil and Spinach Soup

Ingredients

- 2 tablespoons olive oil
- 1 onion, chopped
- 2 carrots, diced
- 2 celery stalks, diced
- 3 cloves garlic, minced
- 1 cup lentils (green or brown), rinsed
- 6 cups vegetable broth
- 2 cups fresh spinach
- 1 teaspoon cumin
- Salt and pepper to taste
- Fresh lemon juice for serving

Instructions

1. **Sauté Vegetables:**
   - In a large pot, heat olive oil over medium heat. Add onion, carrots, and celery; sauté until softened.
2. **Add Garlic and Lentils:**
   - Stir in garlic and lentils; cook for 1 minute.
3. **Add Broth and Seasoning:**
   - Pour in vegetable broth and cumin. Bring to a boil, then reduce heat and simmer until lentils are tender, about 30 minutes.
4. **Add Spinach:**
   - Stir in fresh spinach and cook until wilted. Season with salt and pepper.
5. **Serve:**
   - Ladle into bowls and squeeze fresh lemon juice over each serving.

www.ingramcontent.com/pod-product-compliance
Lightning Source LLC
LaVergne TN
LVHW081619060526
838201LV00054B/2316